Persimmon Sunday

ISBN: 978-0-944048-68-9
purple flag press online at vacpoetry.org/purple-flag
Interior & cover design by Regina Schroeder
Cover image "Persimmon Sunday," ink on paper,
5x7 inches, 2015 © Steven Schroeder

Persimmon Sunday

poems by Ken Hada

Acknowledgments

I am grateful to the editors of the following journals where several of these poems were originally published:

All Roads Will Lead You Home: "September"
Concho River Review: "Only Dreaming"
Illya's Honey: "If not Love, Then," "A Night in Forest," "Like a Fenceless Sky" & "Rainy Morning on the Canadian River"
Malpais Review: "Better Dramas," "Summer Wind," "When Beauty Comes," & "Warblers in May"
Mojave River Review: "Like Hawks above Sage"
Poetry Quarterly: "That Happy Lie" &"Water Splashing on Granite"
Red River Review: "Scissortail at Sunrise" & "Of Rodents and Songbirds" & "Persimmon Sunday"
River Poets Journal: "Snow like This"
Voices de la Luna: "Like First Buds in Spring"

A special thanks to Alan Berecka for his suggestions concerning this collection. I am also grateful to the Faculty Research & Professional Development Committee and Administration of East Central University—Ada, Oklahoma, whose grant afforded me necessary time to complete the collection.

for Tom and Laurie Porter

I. Seems Like Only Crows Survive

II. A Conspiracy of Desire

III. Green and Good, for All It Hides

IV. All is Red, Dark and One

I.

Seems Like Only Crows Survive

Canadian River in Moonlight

Even muddy water shines,
sand glistens—a crystal
menagerie overlooked
in our desperate plight
to dazzle ourselves with wires
and bulbs piling kilowatt
upon kilowatt in the hyper
glow that dulls the faint
hope of progress.

Hear the brackish grass hum
in deeper curves, a salty voice
whispering in shadows—the river
bends forever—follow
the turns toward yesterday.

On the Back Stoop

I stand on the back stoop
in darkness looking up
at stars, tree frogs chortle.

Captive, wayfarer
subdued by enduring wild
unobtrusive glory

I seek an elusive streak
of light to bring me luck.
Like wildlife hidden

in the bush, oblivious
to their numbered days,
my chores keep me

busy surviving beneath
the irrepressible glitter
of late summer night.

Like critters secluded
along sandy shores
I am home.

Like a Fenceless Sky

I wish for the days of coyote-filled nights
when stars were known and you could hear
slow-rising vapor from frosty hollows
or berries on cedar popping to life.

I long to be held like a sleeping child
with tomorrow's dream tucked in a blanket
where loneliness ends like a fenceless sky.

I want to build where nomads are free
to roam and war is no longer fought
for oil or water, where howling with time,
is commonplace, the careful stirring
of coffee at daybreak and yesterday's moon.

Road Building

For three days we cut and scraped
ditches, moved higher piles
of dirt to lower places—dragging,
leveling, smoothing, rounding
in endless cycles up and down
the length, then hitched a weighted
cylinder and rolled for hours packing
the layers firm to receive gravel on top
to withstand rain and snow,
to function, to fulfill a lasting design.

At first I could not see what we
were accomplishing but my tractor
kept moving, kept following dad,
the blade behind, my torso turned,
one arm riding the fender like I knew
what I was doing, revving back and forth,
pulling and pushing dirt, following
dad's s outline of the contours
through pasture shaping a road.

With seventy tons of gravel dumped
we switched implements, geared
down and graded and graded for hours
like sweeping a floor, then packed
and tamped again several more hours
before finish-grading, like frosting
a cake—until he was satisfied each stone
was home nestled solidly together.

The engines spun to quiet—
we climbed down from our perch,
stretched our legs and backs,
heard birds for the first time—
we walked slowly along the road
we had made, the road making us.

August Morning in Drought

Heat glares. Night stays
only a short while.
Already I am hot. Already

the rock patio is brimstone.
Dust floats in lethargic breeze,
a yellow grasshopper clutching

a denim knee of my faded jeans.
I hear a few staggering birds,
see curled leaves and wonder

what it would be like to die
of thirst, to dwindle and dry up
from the inside out—

kind of like the hell
I heard about in childhood
when the evangelist

really got going at fever pitch,
altars lined with lost souls
gulping redemption.

Silence

I take it in sips, like coffee—
morning birds chirping, new sun
through trees—I don't want

absolute moonscape but
I need to hear birds and tree frogs
and crickets and dew

dripping in prairie grass,
a gentle buzz of a grasshopper,
the flutter of dragonflies

soft steps of deer on sand.
I live with interruption—trucks
trudging a road—

I hold my cup, swallow,
close my ears until it is again
safe to taste the morning.

Roadrunner

When I open the back door
he scrambles into brush—
he is welcome here, but
I'm glad he doesn't trust me.

The wild is disappearing.
Maybe this small encounter
doesn't compare with plights
of wolves and whales

but wild is wild, and we must
keep it close. Taming flattens
Earth. Wild thrives with restraint,
respecting limits, knowing

our place. From a distance,
I watch this quick archaic
creature (too cagey to call
friend, too clever to love)

poking grass by the cedars,
spearing grasshoppers, keeping
watch on strangers like me
consuming his prairie.

If Not Love, Then
for Dorothy and Devey

a field languishes
overrun with cedar
cheat grass, sandburs
fire ants and sagging wire
a dusty creek drying
in August sun
breezeless, unrelenting

if not love, then
dingy lights distract
stars which do not matter
since we have no time
to contemplate
their fiery descent, our
place beneath them

indoors we huddle
behind glass, curtains
closed, doors locked
pretending the world stops
at our doorstep
if only we had courage
to open and touch

to sing with morning birds
on the backyard fence
look for crocus lining
the walks, know
chicory and lilac
living among us—
if not love, then

we spin our days never
finding, never holding,
never engaging...
pointless rusting, turning
us inside out—Earth
patiently waiting
our sorry exit

September

...seeping through cracks
of summer—like light
in the barn—dust beams
suspended from ground
to hay loft and beyond—
zones of maze dazzled
children zig through
waving arms, exalting,
pretending—those old
games never get old—
I don't want to lose
the pixie of September...

Patches of Blue

Breaking through leftover gray
laced with golden streaks—I drive
across stale-green landscape
in mid-September trying to avoid
eye contact with trash scattered
in a yard, a brown horse bending
through wire to reach greener
grass—Vivaldi's Concerto in D
helps me see what I feel.

Maybe

I have been placed
here to save me.

Maybe I need to surrender
my dominion of woods,
of fields, their creatures

become a child again
learning to walk
without fear, with faith
(the word sticks in my throat).

If so, I may join you
afloat in the body
of a butterfly in a field
by a creek no one knows.

I don't know how to be
that humble—but maybe
I will learn and perhaps
one day fly meaningfully
about my business

without applause or
notice—the business
of keeping this planet,
remaking myself
in the process.

The Time Between

I will open the back door
step into 4:30 am darkness
breathe the stars hanging low,
time between night and day.

I will again be reminded
of tragedy the way a porch light
obscures the glow
of thousands of megaton stars

some things are too close.

I will think of my father
as the same unbreakable rock

but also how he is changing
how he is now more expressive
than he's ever been—talkative
in revealing, meaningful ways

something we never expected to hear.

Age has a way of opening
a way of turning a rock.

Everyone has an underside
a distant star
despite our tendency to see
only shadow.

Ending Night

Walking before sunrise:

crescent moon, north
breeze—owls
hoo-hoooing softly,

baritone, guttural...
they've been up
all night—now they

call a few last times
sounding tired
as if night has taken

something from them
—a nocturnal calling
not to be denied

their place in an order
determined
by something unseen,

hardly describable.
Venus is just a stone's-
throw from the moon,

fellow stars covered
by sable clouds—
night is about to end.

My slow pulse
connects to unknown
branches set

in forgotten timber
where night birds watch
dark, lonely skies.

A Chill in the Wind

School boys bounce
in broken patterns
but every farmer feels
a chill in the wind.

Grasshoppers flutter
their remaining days,
fewer bird calls—
it is time to travel.

The long road in the sky
is not hard to find
but it does take
some winging to follow.

Flight

The way September wind
rattles cottonwood leaves
a trio of egrets
high above seeking
river sand

occasional honks of geese
cautious vireos
singing the last of summer
a couple of crows keeping
everyone informed

change is in the wind.

I feel my own calling
sharpen my wings
any day now, I too
may take flight.

Cornstalks at Night

The fields are full of secrets.

Murmuring islands
rustling in wind gather
our suspicions.

Green turning gold
in yesterday's sun
now dark
against darker sky
frames a secret world.

Tassels hanging low
crackling in wind
form obscure corridors
where they go to hide

    —whispering
    —whisking
    —witching

       in night wind.

I too imagine things

what I long to be

left out in the cold
hearing footsteps.

Like Hawks above Sage

Something about a prairie
makes you want to follow
flying low like hawks above sage
scattered stalks of bluestem
renegade in late October
too stubborn to die easy
too tough to be anything else.

The wind has ended. Calm
covers like glass, the world
a museum. I would pay
twice to soar once again;
I would pay double to see
from a hawk's eye cruising,
regal, sovereign, fearless.

Though Shadows Accompany

No man loses his shadow except
it is in the night
—Derek Walcott, *Omeros*

A glass of Jameson, pen in hand
I discover a new world, wharfs
and levees submerged by endless sea
creeping in darkness, or swallows
darting all around a church belfry
in October shadows while drivers
pass without notice as if neither
light nor dark moves them
and sundown is just nuisance.

But I will notice. I determined
this long ago, and this dedication
to seeing is my being, my calling.
I will not, not matter. I will not
float like a soggy twig downstream
into darkness unaware. Though
shadows accompany me I will play,
and yes, I will be played.

When Yellow Leaves First Fell

When yellow leaves first fell
across my driveway
I was taken by color
quiet beauty, subtle
in the soil and morning sun
lighting the bordering meadow
soft on caliche and strands
of yellow bunchgrass.

I had no way of knowing
then the days of my autumn
would be a lingering grudge match,
the winner taking death
as its prize. I was too young,
too in love with color
refusing the truth of dead
fallen leaves, gloomy prophets
whose annual appearance
is but a mask for those in line
at the carnival, requisite
to play the game but powerless
to prevent death—beauty
after all, vanishes like clouds
puffed for show, composed
but for a season.

Two Deer in Twilight

Under a favorite pecan tree
days grow shorter—they stay

longer each time. Doe and yearling
duck and dodge, nose in the wind,

skittish eyes shifting. Pecans
prepare them for winter if they live

that long—she remembers shots,
others now gone. How nimble

they must be—every step an epic,
any move could be the last.

Imminent danger makes them
beautiful—taut muscle, coiled

senses—uncanny ability to appear
or to vanish, the envy of ghosts.

First Frost

We knew it would come.
The hay meadow
beneath pecan and elm
lies bare before an unseen
force falling.

Everything bristles.
The world is scarred,
brittle, changed—
under thin pale skin,
a heart hard as stone.

The moon is high
in empyreal sky, the sun
lags behind a hill—death's
chill arrives—seems
like only crows survive.

Persimmon Sunday

I find them beneath my persimmon tree.

They quickly turn to go though
I don't feel like being rough with them.
Fences are necessary, I suppose.
They can be meddlesome too.

These gentle folks pass every Sunday
to visit their boy in prison, they
only want to make a pie. I only want
to be asked first—a fence divides us.

She promises to bring me tarts
and that seems fair, and I think about
fairness and their son these days.
I am glad they go see him Sundays

and I tell them so. Their calm, courtesy
strikes me. Persimmon pie is part of her
autumn ritual, something I cannot deny
her. I don't know, don't need to know

how it is they got off the main road.
They are seeking the sweetness that comes
after the bitterness has ripened.
Standing under a tree none of us really own

I see her boy back home years ago
gleefully eating a piece of pie. I see
her husband proud, happy, the gleam
in her eye, sweet sticky juice sliding

down the boy's dimpled cheeks,
dark eyes aglow as he wipes his mouth
with the sleeve of a flannel shirt
and I want it to be that way again,

want sour taste expunged. Afternoon
gathers and we talk about a hard,
killing frost that makes the sweetness,
a cold harsh night that ripens

this rustic fruit. We shake hands
and I don't look back as I return
through fields where yellow leaves,
orange, dusty, scarlet and intense

lay about me, toss around me
in the breeze that carries ladybugs
unsuspecting toward their graves,
timber standing in reverent silence

as before a judge, as if to judge.
Autumn is the most dramatic
of days—a time to remember
but it is also a time to console.

II.

A Conspiracy of Desire

Moonlight on Frost

Outside my window moonlight
brightens on frost. I think I
hear strings playing—a bass
balances the hope, keeps night

music grounded, major chords
progress in my hearing, but
the moon plays in a minor
key, and I am stuck between

sounds seeking a melody
to be remembered. I think
about deer tonight, how they
huddle in tall grass, soggy

breath exhaling body heat
by a nameless creek bottom,
a communal survival,
and I think about a boy

trying to become a man
playing six-string acoustic
sitting in a chair salvaged
at the Goodwill store, his pride

his throne, a studio where
fingers fret and slide, and peace
finds him, his earnest face, eyes
closed beside a same moonlit

window. What breath, what light
we reflect. What sounds can be known
when death knells and chickadees
scrunch together in cedar.

For All Who Pass By

I saw the future in hunter orange
slowly, stealthily climb the hill
behind the house, his body rocking
from one weighted sidestep to the next
as quiet as possible, heavy
cold-barreled rifle ready, eyes
seeking prey through the morning fog
glistening beneath a slow-rising sun.

I will give this place to him, and he
will give it to his boy—it is our
little slice of dirt where we have been planted

and the child is the father of the man
and a lump rises in my throat, my chest
is a drum—I am only immortal if I give.

I give what I have been given, and giving
gives me the reason I have been seeking
to stand in one place, like old cedars,
gray in pre-dawn shadows, blue-berried
and silent, standing for all who pass by.

Better Dramas

I remember sky frozen gray.
We belly-crawled across pasture
dragging shotguns to a cedar break
huffing thin air trying hard not to spook
geese on the pond.

I remember brutal, cold days.
We stalked through bunchgrass,
ragweed and plum thickets following
a dog on point to flush wild quail.

Those days are gone.

Most of those who hunted with me
are gone—their children have grown
into rabid right-wingers hating the president's
socialism—forgetting their ancestral lands
were a government gift in the Land Runs
and were saved by FDR and sustained
by subsequent years of federal farm acts
that paid them not to plow, protecting
their markets from a free economy.

I miss frosty mornings.
We knew that if we hung in there
sun would eventually thaw us.

We seemed more thankful then.

Sometimes I sit on the porch smoking
in frigid air and hear distant geese
honking in mid-winter flight and consider
how easy it is to speak the words—
Self-Reliance—back then

I did not think we would grow up
to be belligerent white men who assume
the rules don't apply to us.

Back then we loved better dramas—
the boy reliving rituals
of the frozen prairie under endless,
merciful sky.

Monster Buck

His shadow in the evening sun appears
bigger than I expect, his looming presence
entrances me. I cannot break the spell.

I suppose the wind is still whirling
through oak limbs above me. I do not

recognize twigs falling, leaves floating,
crows quietly disappearing, songbirds
suddenly mute, squirrels still as mice.

I cannot breathe. I cannot keep my heart.
I am collapsed into a vacuum of exalted
terror, suspended in stupor that reminds
me of our shared and tenuous blood.

Chaparral

The ground is turning white—
freezing rain covers the sandy patches
where fire ants and grasshoppers carved
space in the wild grass, post oaks
stand silent, clinging brown dead
leaves collect the falling ice.

I feel high when cold comes,
when the pressure drops and change occurs
before my eyes—I don't need to believe
the unseen, a relief for an apostate
who enjoys the tragedy of autumn,
the arrival of winter.

Tucked in my big blue chair
browsing good books, I turn pages slowly,
paper touching fingertips—Graham Parsons
and Emmy Lou singing softly, a stiff cup
of coffee set in the window sill steams
the glass. I wonder where wild birds
have sheltered—I'm pretty sure
I'll smoke a cigar today.

Returning Snow

Like magic dad pushed snow
until it became a ball
which he patted firm as he rolled
it over and over
until it became a bigger ball—
too big for me to believe.

He rolled snow into three balls
(with some clumsy help from us kids)
then he sat one ball on top of another
until a body emerged and we
began to understand—our eyes

opened, we searched for the best rocks
to make eyes, a carrot nose, broom handle
for arms —
                    arms that still reach
out to us, like a Christ, frozen in concrete
on a mountain unmoving, unmovable

or like a mother—until transformation
occurred and the magic dissipated,
left us wondering what happened,
where it all went and why it had to go.

Snow like This

It was a snow like this
when I fell in love
with your mother.

We skipped class
and took a long walk
through the park.

Trees seemed taller,
bold flakes covered us
like a blanket

landing on her eyelids,
rosen cheeks, wonder
in her eyes, her

raven hair a riveting
contrast to the white
falling all over her.

We stood on a bridge
looking down at gray
water unmoving.

Cedars in Snow

Sprawling limbs never bare,
on this morning snow
sticks to their broadness.

The branches accented
like an artist might paint
—shadow and light.

The things we take on
color us, a canvass
suitable for framing.

Laughing the Devil Away

Snow makes me think of others:
an ensemble in a country store
playing dominos around a pot-belly stove

a family before a fireplace at home
dreaming, warm and nostalgic

or children with their fathers rolling down
a hill, sledding, plodding, pretending
to be angels laughing the devil away.

Snow makes me think of others:

on days when the devil is my only companion
I think of you and thank the snow
for falling fast—the glee of my voice
bouncing across a hill, parka zipped
all the way up, stocking cap pulled tight
around my ears, cold air poking
at the bare space between my sock
and pant leg—hot breath, numb fingers.

Do you miss those cold days,
what they did for us back then
when angels and devils played together?

Winter Comes to El Chaparral

Death hovering—foreboding
sky falling—freezing
killing rain
followed by suspicious snow

an owl

white as earth looks down
from white sycamore limbs
over silence too vast
too white for words—

                timid
pale sun, a plaintive voice
of a pileated—by sundown
several birds gather in topmost
branches of a hackberry,
rabbit tracks leading
to underbrush.

Of Rodents and Songbirds

Winter takes over—white snow covers
yellow grass the color of chicken broth
served in a pea-green bowl inside walls
where fear and contentment hold truce
in mutual respect of death.

The beauty of a snowy morning mixed
with the dread of zero temperatures
sways at the mercy of fragile electricity.

How close we are to rodents and songbirds
cloistered in knots of scattered brush, ice
drops frozen in place, crusty snow covering
hidden lairs—tiny hearts beating at fever
pace just to survive—something unseen,
something rarely considered.

Radio reports the death of Nelson Mandela,
too quickly recounts his life, his incarceration,
quotes his call for forgiveness...
                                    here
on the frigid, white, southern plains
the news seems foreign and faded
like a bent photograph found in a shoebox
tucked away in a closet, an aging, displaced
postcard from the other side of the world.

Candle-flame flickers. I look out windows
across white pasture, feel winter in my bones
and see the death only beauty forgives.

In a Field Where Even Time Freezes

White sky falling, uncountable,
unfathomable pieces flaking

flooding ground in morning haze,
white clouds hanging low

dumping snow by the barrel,
blowing, assaulting

everything is covered, nothing
escapes the soft fury.

Through the torrent a cardinal
calls a couple of notes—

imperceptible, his voice sounding
odd in the silent storm.

I don't know what he wants, what
he means. This is how beauty

comes, the way song rises in notes
unexpected in places

thought void, lifeless. But what I hear
must be remembered

even if unknown, misunderstood.
I hear you. Yes, I hear

you. Do you know how important
that is? How necessary

for me to hear color live again
this bleached morning?

Winter at Ve'theuil: Monet Painting Camille

Like Monet painting his young, dying wife
art surprises in ways we cannot predict
or control, even if we have nerve to try.

Her deathbed becomes his studio,
so unlike her sunny walk in the field
with a parasol, this wife, this mother
blending with ghostly, ghastly grays
and blues accompany her at the end,
an irreverent morning sun provides
the only color, just enough light
for us all to see what he is losing.

In helpless languor, he can do little else
but compose her fading likeness. The gory
impressionism so keenly befits death,
for how can one represent the loss of life,
what is a greater distortion than death—
the declining body, the withering face?
In broad, fragmented blotches of colorless paint
death becomes manageable.

In days surrounding her death Monet
painted Ve'theuil in the Mist and Ice Floes—
the jagged, ice-jammed river of grief,
a lack of clarity surrounding him, dire winter
scenes gripping him, the sunny meadow
with his lady strolling lightly in bright pastel,
now only a lost memory.

On that fateful morning, his young wife
dead before him, his brush obeys
impulsive grief, and I feel his despair
sitting there, bedside, losing her,
without money, with two children,
with critics mocking his style—what is one

to do but cry out for relief, or as only
Monet could do, take up his brush and paint
her tender face shrouded in the breath
of winter. He painted her—like a draught
animal working at the millstone—he
later confided to a friend—the artist
a servant, a responding ox, he paints
her tragic temples drawing taut
in the brutal death blows of winter,
everything is lost, her body covered
by the grim obtuseness we can only feel,
her mouth turned down to meet eternity
with a frown, her closed eyes save her
from watching him, her husband, paint her.
She is reduced now, dwindling, one last study,
her pose is perfect for his angry strokes—here
art dare not imitate life, for life so precious
and so terrible blows away so suddenly,
like the brumal force they both feel it to be.

Grasping (Like Fingers Infant, Desperate)

Loneliness is hunger
hidden, a force
that surprises even
after all this time

grasping (like fingers
infant, desperate)
pale notes of survival
stinging joy with terror.

How we bleed
and what we need
are firmly gripped
in a conspiracy of desire.

Broken Limbs

The way ice breaks limbs,
wind shakes them to the ground
it is easy enough to believe
that someone or something failed

but for some reason broken limbs
don't really bother me.

They seem ironic, artistic
like driftwood on a beach
like scars on the face of a shrimper
or an old cowboy, the places
razor stubble resist...

like a bent and stained windmill
useless in a place where water
no longer rises, where wind
is powerless to turn the corrupted tin.

I seem to be one of those limbs
twisted in place, shaken by wind
with only the memory of greener days.
Maybe it is this graying life
that fits us best.

Shivers

Being hated
being not loved
bores all the way to bone.

Like animals in cold
deep night keep moving
just to keep moving.

She could not see
her past
in her future.

I walked away
dragging my heart
like road-kill

trying
to look both ways
at the same time.

Fog

The remaining snow is sloppy white
stained with seeping red dirt.

Gray skies dropping around me
yet I am rising—at home in fog,
unclear lines blurring me.

This singing sky I hear I believe,
this joyful off-key attempt
at harmony, flat and unrecognized,
unrecognizable, I applaud and sweep
the front porch of a quiet home.

I cross a river adrift in ethereal
elements that drive me indoors
humming anew those same old tunes.

III.

Green and Good, for All It Hides

Canadian River: Purple Dawn

The bridgework at Asher nears
completion but water below,
coursing sand, needs no upgrade.

The timeless stream tugs
at me every morning I cross.
Nothing changes but light and my

limited ability to see. I see no tracks
in sand, no coyote creeping
the shores, no swallows darting

no hawks circling the somber sunless
sky, no cranes sticking upright
in shallows, no mallards clustered

in the river's turn. But I hear
the music of what I cannot see—
the river in motion is cleaner

than strings on a Martin guitar,
brighter than any score
composed by Brahms or Bartok.

Antlers

Antlers from a young buck
fallen by a spry sumac,
decaying oak leaves
piled alongside.

How strange he felt
when spikes first poked
from his gallant skull,
how hard he rubs
a few months later

to remove calloused
cartilage from his bloody
scalp—how short-lived
the glory of the rut.

Like First Buds in Spring

On a path in piney woods
you stood beside your dad
facing the camera trying
to be all grown up in waders
too big for ten-year old
shoulders, a flyrod twice
as long—
                    that look
on your face is not just
uncertainty of what may
or may not be caught
in a mountain stream.

Pondering your hunched
shoulders, puzzled eyes
I see love like first
buds in spring—
                    and I know
flowers fade far too soon,
far too soon.

In Crumbs Most Vital

There are words to keep
me living, words
I have yet to hear
you speak.

Until then I read
your face, shoulders,
the crease in your neck,
a dimpled smile

curling at surprising
times in ways
I keep. I tell myself
to be content.

I am not the first man
who must translate
the vulgar to find
what is lost

in crumbs most vital,
appeasements
precluding my hunger
for validation.

Fallen Limbs

I thank the ice for breaking
these limbs, dropping
them from the family tree.

I bend, pick up fallen limbs
a handful at a time, feel
bark in my fingers, sunny

wind on my neck, red
mud sticking to my boots.
I carry brokenness

uphill, aware of my steps
to a severed, scattered pile
waiting to be burned.

Today, bearing the broken
is enough—the bending,
the lifting, the touching...

Silence Coming Down like Rain

It is hardest to bear alone,
pulsating against an empty drum
while the meaning of things
hardens until they are too soft
to withstand the assault.

Make yourself an instrument.
Play darkness—
avoid words like loneliness,
authenticity, hope.

Bend your shoulders, bear
silence coming down like rain.

In This Silent, Drab Place

These yellow buds
on green stems
seem lost, like they
don't belong

in this silent
drab place where color
feels foreign.

Crusted and course
the ochre soil
reminds me of myself

suspicious
of something new.
These springing flowers
intrigue me.

In a Leafless Tree near Sundown

When spring comes to old men
their eyes see again what they
have been missing, young men
become nervous—the storied
power of old bulls turning
pastures into paradise
rings in their boyish ears

but for now the moon apexes
far above the treeline
and all I see is the dirt
beneath my fingernails
while light crescendos
and conquers me with sound
unsingable—a chorale

far too real for imitation
floating around ambition
where stars and water
blur together in horizons
that beckon like a dream
despite the silence
despite the dirt that forms us

frames our hope of beauty.
I sing the glory of pollen
drifting in air, swollen eyes
and uplifted hearts
are the tell-tale signs
that we die a little more
each day we survive.

Just yesterday a Tanager
in a leafless tree
near sundown staked
his claim to a limb with song
and tonight before moonrise
a pregnant doe grazes
tiny sprouts yet unseen.

Rainy Morning on the Canadian River

The way the clouds cluster into clumps
darker layers covering dark layers
decorate a course of river, grays
and blues hovering above ready sand
a triumph of art in the wilderness.

Look upstream with me and read
the proofs slowly falling toward
an unseen sea—the sage reaching
sandy shores—scattered raindrops
sweeping pastures nearby.

Pebbles

I don't know if time
heals all wounds
or not.

Colors tend to fade
but ripples
only rebound

and return
revolving cycles
that never seem to end.

If pain is like that
I can only hope
so is the salve—

a growing tree,
a blues horn,
an unpretentious pup—

these little blessings
like pebbles
in surging current.

Fleeting

We are drawn to a meadow
trimmed in grand green trees,
yellow hay bales rolled
to order at rest in evening sun
like angels guarding holy fields,

We were made for beauty
no matter how fleeting—
and isn't it amazing that beauty
tends to find us when we fail
when we are distracted?

A prayer might simply be
that each life gets a glimpse,
a moment to pose, to be
and to be painted, something
to carry in the coming days.

Man in a Blue Smok
after Cézanne, 1896

How earnest he is wearing
his necessary hat with little
else to show for his labor,
his ungarnished life painted
in round, uncertain shoulders,
fingers tapping in his lap—

but a heart reaching—dark
eyes daring to meet fear
with determination in this one
moment. Around his neck
a red scarf—color which he
has yearned his whole life.

That Happy Lie
after Bouguereau's Shepherdess

It's her hair, after all
that keeps my eyes fixed past
her curves, her green skirt, arms
hands, shoulders that cradle
her favorite found stick
worn smooth into a staff
that has corralled, carries
life more than I can know.

This idyllic temptress
rivals King David, eyes
refusing to reveal
secrets of starry skies,
her unflinching gaze, feet
bare in the soil that she
embodies. This un-kept
saint is nobody's fool.

It's her hair, after all
that seduces. See it
tossed in bucolic breeze,
tussled just right to tame
a continent yet wild
enough for onlookers
to believe that happy
lie called Arcadia.

Toward Midnight
for Sally Rhoades

Walk with me up and down
the only hill I know,
side-stepping briars
under silent, pewter sky

your pants tucked in
my borrowed gray socks
in my oversized boots
like snow-shoeing

Adirondack winters.
We saunter brown leaves
and broken limbs—
your voice through trees

like glowing wind
carries seeds of friendship,
sowing our way
toward midnight.

What I Cannot Do

I cannot make you love
the way rain dripping
from April sky
sharpens redbuds
like lasers dissecting
a heart with precision
a surgeon envies

a fiery fuchsia
glowing against gray
skies and drizzled bark
scattered in the brush

but I can show you
new clover as small
as drops of water
bright as an emerald
sun, under cover
of dead winter grass.

Scissortail at Sunrise

Scissortail on Easter
Sunday sunrise
sitting a wire
like a Christ returning

an artist painting sky
safe for mammals
and disciples
of fork-tailed deity.

Time for worship:
the empty tomb
is but one song
the choir of heaven sings.

April in Passing

The Elm tree is nearly full
again—new leaves
completing the return—

alone in winter, the bare
trunk and branches
now welcome back the green—

relationships need mending-
I need leaves green
and good for all it hides.

Sunday Morning in April

Wind roars through gullies
and gulches. It is Sunday morning
in April. You can hardly hear

the voices of birds slicing
this furious, darkening day—
a day that recalls other

April Sundays in Oklahoma
when wind and dust vented
their stormy marriage

on those standing by helplessly
watching, waiting for sky
to lighten, for clouds to pass.

We bow our heads. Though prayer
seems futile, it feels natural,
so impulsively necessary—but my,

listen to the persistent birds
singing through venomous air,
chirping up to the moment

of devastation. They will not be
outdone by wind. They will be here
when everything else blows away.

Whippoorwill through the Storm

The persistent calling carries through
dark timber, treetops swaying,
thunderheads boiling above,
humidity crowding us, making
us edgy—the milk cow swishing
her tail, stomping her leg, overturns
the pail spilling its contents,
black flies buzzing like Baptists
longing for Armageddon.

Tonight the sky is a spurned woman.
Kali rides the bitter clouds
while Timber Rattlers and King
Snakes cross the highway, June Bugs
buzzing the kitchen window

Through chaos, the Whippoorwill,
steady as a drummer, keeps my nerves
in place, and I feel that surviving
is worth the effort.

Soundings

Sounds in the morning:

birds hidden in trees
or lined on fences a half-mile away

truck tires humming on a highway

and Shirley Horn's voice sounding
oddly familiar—this jazz-singing
night owl heard at sunrise, a book of James
Wright poems, black coffee
                      an awareness
of how sound means.
There is no poem
you can write to portray the turkey hen
feeding in the far shade of a pasture
hunting in shadows of cottonwoods
pecking the ground like an old Greek sailor
taking his soundings.

We seek to survive.

The sun and the shade become one
in our tenuous journey

and I hear the voice of God
clearing his throat.

Warblers in May
after Myriam Fraga

Duke Ellington's swing band starts
Tuesday morning. Coffee and chicory,
New Orleans style, helps me find

the back stoop. I unlock the door, step
into timeless sage and hardwoods.

Hear the warblers. Stop. Listen close.
Marvelous trilling every horn player mimics.

Sit with me, won't you? Sit with me
in the first streaks of light. Let's sit
a good long while, what's the hurry?

Everything moves too fast. We've hijacked
ourselves, hostage to ransom we cannot pay.

Our boat tumbles in the waves. Clinging
to a capsizing boat, we survive because we are lucky.
In the waves we promise to be better...

Sit with me a while.
Sit and listen
to the warblers in May.

IV.
All is Red, Dark and One

Like Sediment, We Seem To Accept
for Josh Grasso

and he hums medleys of old but
forgotten days
—Chekhov , *Ward No.6*

Living in the past
has its charm
and who is to say memory
is not a comfort
or even a corrective?

But madness is close
to nostalgia—the perilous ways
we misremember, the feel good
of days gone by
like sediment, we seem to accept
as truth, but if we cut
open the earth and look
not down but sideways
we can see layer upon layer
packed tightly, a distinct
structure below the surface.

Excavation, on occasion
is worth the effort.
Friends, get out your shovel,
hum a merry tune and dig.

When Beauty Comes

You may be alone at midnight
under countless stars
sprinkling the doorstep of heaven
thick dew dousing the grass
leaves hanging heavy in silence

You may be a thirteen-year-old boy
listening for rock-n-roll on a transistor
bought with money made hauling hay
only to discover late in the night
in the secrecy of your room
some station playing classical music
from a far-off, imagined place

You may be my lover unbuttoning
a comfortable cotton blouse, stepping
naked into a shower surrounded
by candles sweetly moaning, warm
water caressing your curved shoulders

You may be holding an infant son
his mouth gaping like a fish, seeking
a milky nipple, tiny fingers grasping
yours forever bound by birth
groping in darkness familiar flesh
that can never be untouched

Only Dreaming

How little I want but the drumbeat
of a Downy Woodpecker
keeping time Sunday morning
with streaks of pink coloring the clouds
above native grass and sunflowers

two cups of coffee, recall sipping
bourbon late at night with Lucinda
Right in Time—Lake Charles—Jackson—
Car Wheels on a Gravel Road—

accordion riffs come back to me
like new sun through cottonwoods

Still I Long for Your Kiss—Don't
want nothin if I have to fake it—

Redbirds Balancing on Cedar Limbs

How can I expect anything more
than what I ask of myself
in these days of transition, these nights
alone, and the wind comforts
in the oddest ways?
                              Sometimes I hope
to dream forever, to never wake
where green grass and leaf-filled trees
harbor birds beyond measure.
                              Their song
is a temporary fix, something
to keep other things away.

If I wake to yellow sun in white morning,
redbirds balancing on cedar limbs
then I will know the dream has not failed.

Pecan Tree

If you know the joy holding
a pecan tree in half-tone, light
and softer light, I don't see
how you could ever let it go.

As it should be—the glow
grows dim, turn by turn, and I
wait with expectation
for the shadow to reach my

toes dipping in the pool
of residual light, a French horn
and clarinet in harmony—
the song I wish I could sing.

Water Splashing on Granite

Sometimes beauty cuts so deep
I can see clear through
to what is not there.

In this absence I see myself
most clearly, and know you
for what you are not.

We receive the sublime sometimes
unwittingly, but when the human
part glimpses that which was

and that which is to come,
in a moment, we know the curse
of attraction and the blessing

of the ordinary. Water splashing
on granite cuts a bank all the way
to the ocean and back

and like a fool I curse the rain.

A Night in Forest

These pines are taller
than I remember.
On my back at campsite
I look up dazed, distant.

August sun warms sky
and water lightly tapping
rocks of this tiny island
in some Canadian wilderness.

Night vanishes—a wolf's
cry fades like a gun shot
into silent abyss. At
water's edge my canoe

rests in gentle new
daylight—no more rocking
on bow and stern, upside
down in dark breezes.

Back Channel

Some things can only be discovered.

Not every path, not every stream
is mapped—there behind a stand
of salt grass high as your head find
an opening, a way through sand
over gravel—
                          follow the water
where it wants to go—it cannot be
stopped—
                          how to get around
the obvious, to remain obscure but
vital—this overlooked world governed
by stray water is as needed as sun
and rain. It is everything I want.

I return to this bulrush from time
to time to reunite with the sand and birds.
I stay until I am finally obligated to rejoin
the mainstream to flow within the force
of others bending to the stars, so full
of ourselves, immersed in power—

but I must not forget this place that found
me—those days are mine. They made me
as I am—and if I understand rivers,
the unacknowledged carry the blood
of the world as we circle to the sea.

Hooked

after Boy on the Creek
Charles Banks Wilson

The waters have receded
leaving wraithlike roots exposed.
The great trees of summer
endure and fish find a hole
in the bend of a creek.

The boy's back arching, setting
the hook, pole bending, there is
no attention like this—
no world, no tomorrow.
Everything past has vanished

confirmed in surprise. Not much
beats a fish on a hook.

Symphonies in the Bush, Raw and Timeless

If not a flute, violins bend
with the river through cliff
and crevice, strings entwined
with bluestem and salt-grass
at water's edge, melancholy
measures over rocks dripping
rhythms, swirling, swishing
toward harmony, bouncing
across sandy rises and gravel
bars, oaks and fellow trees.

Before recording machines,
before paper, before river cane
was cut, hollowed and holed
to sound like canyon wind
symphonies in the bush, raw
and timeless filled the silence,
raised our slumbering selves
until we sensed something
we might become, something
we might have been.

Quail

In the sundown
of a canyon
somewhere beyond
sight his voice stings
the empty air.

Nothing but wind
answers in those
dark intervals
filled with silence,
nothing returns.

Soliloquy

Faded jeans fit him
like skin on a deer.
He walks with shuffling boots
sensing his own primacy.

A cousin lost in the city
named for a grandfather
he never knew

he is a quail
lost in brush, only a memory
of a covey
                    a song no one hears

star on the stage of his making
            a playhouse
            no cover charge
            no usher
            no playbill
just the recoil of nature.

Like willows endlessly trying

to right themselves
after ice and wind push them
down to an earth

                    they remember.

Full Moon

The earth is somersaulting!
If I don't fall off I feel
I will have accomplished

something. Cedars and oak
have roots but I am
floating in space, tumbling

in a vacuum into which
I was born, destiny
that catapults

its way to the other side.
If I land upright I can't
take credit, I had lots

of help. This inertia
I've heard about is real
and success is just

a joyful turn of the wheel,
as is failure, but who
can remember that when

you are upside down believing
you are right-side up
and neither is really true?

Gloomy-Eyed Bastards Who Clearly Saw

We once believed that witches
had kinship with the moon, some corrupt,
vile union that kept old hags
linked to the supernatural, a dark
and odious humor illumined
by lesser light—digging roots,
black bile, bloody séances—all that
morbid and magic melancholy.

And here I am—alone and writing
under a bright waxing moon—the sweep
of light so tremendous the shadows
linger, alive with superstition
ghosts haunting all around me.
I guess it is my time of the month.

Will they burn a poet at the stake
like they once tortured prophets
thought to be false, those gloomy-
eyed bastards who clearly saw
the underside of the holy club,
a god-ordained bourgeoisie
congratulating its pious self
by lamplight behind locked doors
while evil paraded in the woods?

These days I'm afraid poets portend
the obvious. Tame, nothing ugly
about us, we long to be mainstream.
Loved by the others, we want the moon
for a decal, a marketing ploy
to exploit insecure postulants

lined like dull ducks on a stagnant pond
at brightest day, a baptismal font
for novices on a pretty lawn
where witch hazel and sassafras root
could never be imagined.

The Puritans expunged them
though we still fear dark outdoors, cedar
and cottonwood looming in the realm
of the unclean and the damned.

Yet I hear the wings of whizzing bats
doing thankless work. In the glow
of distorted perception I wait
sniffing the cultic breeze with cigar
and Irish whiskey, this calm council
of the empty prairie, endless sky.

In moonglow, un-rhyming sorcerers
laugh at the superstition of fools
who cannot abide the complete life.

Tonight I feel myself a fellow
darkling, sibling to yesterday's charm—
an incubus with pen and paper
playing and praying in the beaming
conduit that unifies the real
with the imagined, a universe
forever smoldering in darkness.

This lonely office, these tools
of my trade, a journal as shovel,
I dig to unearth the rotting vines
disguised in the soil we fear to love,
ironic verse—fire falling in sky.

When Coyotes Howl

Even the dogs hush.

We cannot help but look back
over our shoulder
when old voices echo
in marrow not felt in years.

Dark wind carries wild dirges
across prairie miles so effortlessly
you can taste the acridity ...

and you are never the same.

These tame dogs lazing around me
chained and indifferent
grow sullenly fierce
by what they fear to see

but wildness is no diviner,
no referee of the soul.

Smell its pungent fur thick
on the nape of your neck
and wonder what made you as you are,
who will claim you as you might have been.

Glistening teeth shine fierce,
so ferocious the moon swivels,
plummets like a doomed kite—
a mere toddler—helpless, round and soft.

Prairie Home

after Elizabeth Raby's
Ransomed Voices

We know we are soft.
We don't dig wells by hand
plow ground behind a mule
build houses from sod.

Now we live fat and secure
the victims of our minds
that have polished
our lives into souvenirs.

Would you want the scrabble
of our fore-mothers
the calloused grind
our fathers endured?

What would you give
in exchange for their plight?
What would you be
if the world failed

to comply with your hands
if your feet weary
and bleached balked
from hope the way a mule

balks in the presence
of a snake? We talk
about strength and honor
and determination

like they are recent
inventions, new formulas
conceived in laboratories
for the blessed.

We have that luxury
don't we? Even birth
was too often a curse
where survivors

strain to hear a faint
echo from Eden.
Death is unopposed
even welcomed

when the marrow
finally dissolves
and endless wind stalks
us, stacks us

like empty husks.
It is just the way
we survive
remembering the good

and the strong.
It is just the way we
soften into progress.

When I Am Dying

...if I say I am dying, / within this finite
life enclosed at either end / by the
unknowable, what are my words
—B.H. Fairchild, *Wittgenstein, Dying*

Sun through cedar marks
me like lattice work,
an irregular
wavering crossword
puzzle in morning
that seems without end.

What could be more un-
certain than dying?
Birds peck grass seed sown
just yesterday, their
concord is sometimes
more than I can stand.

When I am dying
Shirley Horn soothes me
with soft-sweeping snares—
honey from the bee—
looming brass echoes
just foolin' myself—

Such bold cabaret
was never certain
in any final sense,
but isn't this what birds
and seeds of grass
already know?

The Heaven I Thought I knew
after David Bates: Self-Portrait
—Grassy Lake—Fall, 2004

Scarlet, virile and brown
dark and final surrounding me

there is no color
that is not falling, blending
to oak—daunting, a final passage
returning to a womb
I could not have known, or
is it just the sky indistinguishable
from the dirt-dug and narrowed grave?

The only color is my forest green
canoe—I sit still in torpid dusk
as heaven closes its door—the bow
of my boat, like my future,
is just a few feet beyond me
and yet unfathomable—the dying
light—
                    I sit tight, paddle
at rest on my bent knee, my white
shirt covering my heart—the last light
I will know.

I have paddled a lifetime in this lake.
Every stroke has brought me
to this stopping point where, with eyes
still aware, I arch my back, look
one last longing time over bowed
shoulders at the heaven I thought
I knew—red darkness is all—all is red,
dark and one.

Summer Wind

Down abandoned tracks
I knew in younger days
follow a path once live
with commerce

now just more evidence
of time passing:
Money rises, money falls,
but the Sycamore
along the river, the Hackberry
and Oak do not fade,
are not fooled by the false front
called progress.

When a boy follows
a whim whispering in summer
wind there is nothing to do
but follow and years
later, I still feel humidity
sticking to scant clothes
the humus-rich atmosphere
filling my senses.

I hear a Cardinal deep
in the woods.
It is enough;
It is everything.

About the Author

Ken Hada is the author of six collections of poetry. His work has been featured around the country including four times on The Writers' Almanac. Recipient of the 2011 Wrangler Award from the Western Heritage Museum, Ken's books have twice been named finalist for the Oklahoma Book Award, as well as a finalist for the 2015 Spur Award. Reviews of his work and other information may be found at www.kenhada.org

CPSIA information can be obtained
at www.ICGtesting.com
Printed in the USA
LVHW041721040219
606320LV00003B/693/P